AF367362

years of soul songs, love, and tender musings

Christopher deLellis

Love Poems for the Soul
published by Christopher deLellis, USA
This book is also available as eBook.

This is a work of fiction. The characters, events, and locations portrayed in this book are fictitious. Any similarity or resemblance to actual events, locales or persons, living or dead, is entirely coincidental and not intended by the author.

First published 2021

© 2021, all rights remain with the author
© 2021, cover design by Katharina Kolata, Independent Bookworm
© 2021, cover background by rfphoto, Depositphotos
© 2021, cherry blooms by silvionka, Depositphotos
© 2021, cherry trees by norwayblue, Depositphotos
© 2021, abstract flower by lyudo, Depositphotos
© 2021, zen-lotus by dampoint, Depositphotos

printed by IngramSparks LLC, 1 Ingram Blvd.
LaVergne, TN. 37086, USA, www.ingramspark.com

ISBN-13 978-3-95681-229-3

Table of Contents

Chapter 4: Passion

Foreword

The flower of my soul has always beckoned me toward the light it seeks. Poetry created the rich and fertile soil that perpetually lead me to that light.

In my late teens and early twenties, I was easily swept into the ever-changing river of love. In San Francisco in the tumultuous Seventies, surrounded by wonderful poets and great teachers, my poetry was filled with passions of a young man.

Romanticism, and poets who brazenly spoke of desire and love, held my attention. I began writing very romantic poems to more completely express the joy and elation of the delicious relationships I was experiencing.

As I matured, and deepened my spiritual connection, I found richer textures and more vibrant colors that helped me give expression to a profounder understanding of love. In those latter years, this deepening served to shape many of the poems in this book.

The poems in this pocket book were selected from over a thousand poems I've written, throughout many years. I hope you will find that some of them will touch you, and give a glimpse of the enduring impressions my experiences of love have left on my soul.

Chapter 1
God and the Universe

A Tribute
to the Sound of Love

May the sound of love come into your heart,
like a warm ocean wave caressing the shore,
gently washing this *forever* love into your soul.

May the joy of love spread from your spirit,
in sacred chants, flowing like a river of stars,
becoming the unfolding of your divine gifts.

And, as you breathe out the sound of your bliss,
the song of your eternal Love will abound infinitely.

Asking the Universe

I wait in silent clarity, and exquisite anticipation,
for a glimpse of this twin flame that binds my soul.
I sit in deep meditation breathing in the texture of her kiss,
imagining her gentle hands so sensuously against my cheeks.
I listen softly to the music of desire,
hypnotized by her fragrant embrace.

Wanting to draw her magic, sketch her eloquence with my mind,
sculpt her with these longing eyes, those so magnificent shapes.
Begging the Universe to grant me just one more tomorrow,
just one more taste of her lips and the sound of her voice.
Asking to let me linger just a little while longer under her spell.

Before the Beginning of Time Parable

Before the beginning of time,
there was a singular Sun,
that shone bright for billions of years
without a single thought but to shine
with a light that only the Sun knew.
But there came a time when that singular Sun
began to have second thoughts.

And in particular, a new thought began to appear.
This lead to the awakened consciousness.
The conscious Sun began to embrace the possibility of
something "else" quenching the thirst
of now-discovered essential longing,
the hallowed sense of desire for another
just as brilliant light.

And after several million years of evolving,
the Sun, in its new consciousness,
began co-creation with the Universe of Love.
And in another hundred thousand years or less,
there was born another brilliant light, a second Sun.
And from this union, the Moon came into existence.
And the Moon had a singular purpose…
to reflect the magnificent light of the duel suns.

Concert at Dawn

In these early morning hours
the sky and water
blend into one another
at the horizon's edge
mixing with soft gray clouds
making a fog-layered cocktail
that rises from the cool waters
all uniting in a gift of incredible blues
celebrating the magnificence of yet
another miraculous new day.

Oh, how good it feels to drink deep
into the ocean of that joyous sound
and breathe in whole-heartedly
the grandeur from sky to ground
that is pulsing in this planet effortlessly
and to realize almost unknowingly
God's universal concert is all around.

Divine Intervention

I saw you standing there so perfect
in the smoke-filled bar one late afternoon.
A goddess, behind an ancient counter,
you, as magnificent as a harvest moon.

And after several attempts of pure determination,
I tried pulling your eyes to the far end of the room.
And locked in some unexpected intention of awareness,
I endeavored, time and time again, to get your attention.

Finally, you "saw me" scribbling passionately on a napkin,
and in the soft light stillness, you stopped making drinks,
momentarily smiled delightfully my way at last, only
two or three seconds, but for me, it felt like eternity.

So, I wrote and wrote down words of my heart's desire,
signing my name and added my soul's mark, a simple flower.
And the rest is filled with years and years of waiting, until at last,
the remarkable reunion, given I'm convinced, by divine
    intervention.

Souls

Like water in this Ocean of Love,
all souls travel inside temples of shell.
Some coupled on this magnificent journey,
soaring and diving as dolphin-like companions.
Others, drifting alone upon self-made rafts,
until finally, all of us reach that same place,
where all souls are returned to Oneness.

We bear witness to all that is Sacred,
on the narrow path of trust and belief,
for as long or short, our earthly journey.
Bring your Self then, raveling barefoot
onto the soft and merciful ground.

We watch the stories inside dreams unfold,
blessed images of magnificent birds soaring,
like golden-winged spirits, flying effortlessly
just above the clouds of our prayers.

Timid, we wait, anxious for the unfolding truth,
the reverent notes whistling in the Four Winds.
Or sitting in meditation, breathing in the All,
we ask questions of why, and how come,
until the sacred teacher whispers soft and clear,
answering all questions locked inside our shells.

Finding Joy Within

I felt her joy and the magnificent tugging on my hands,
sensed that exquisite divine connection happening again.
God whispered inside me "Let your inner voice to burst forth!"
I knew the richness of being Love, complete in my heart's
    overflowing.

And I rejoice, as the chosen beneficiary of this splendidness,
witnessing her in the divine dance of Heart and Soul.
I am blessed, and brought into this quiet stillness,
finding the joy she brings forth, and I carry joyfully within
    my soul.

The Eye of God

"His eye fell upon me cold and fiery"
The tunnel – hollow socket -
drew me to its very end,
where an infinitesimal golden light flickered.

Dying, feeling a last breath,
I reached out to touch the source,
but the light exploded,
rocketing me backward a thousand years,
where I fell once again into the earth.

The Stained-Glass Window on Mission Street

I walked toward the cathedral on Mission Street,
noticing one of the magnificent stained-glass windows
quake-fallen, and shattered on the street.
Shards and beautiful fragments of all colors sparkled,
in the strong and brilliant early afternoon's light.

I hung my head in despair and solemn grief,
as I almost absently starting to walk past
the magnificent St. Patrick Catholic Church.
But, as I glanced up into that sharp sun,
the doors were wide open and inviting me in.
So, I stepped inside, tentative and unsure,
and walked to the altar and stood in awe.

As the light broke through all those amazing iconic images,
I was consumed in light and felt so composed and clear.
It was then I realized, we are all stained-glass windows.
But we can only truly be seen, when in deep reverence,
we allow ourselves to be fully bathed in the Creator's light.

This Love Could Last Forever

I know this love could last forever,
listening, as your voice rises in glorious song.
And every time I see your soul smiling out loud,
or sit in silence watching your heart dance,
the more clearly I can understand words like divine.

I know this love could last forever,
every time I step into this river of exquisite love,
and all the times we dive so joyously
into the magnificent ocean of our connection.
Swimming effortlessly in each other's glow,
I'm reassured, by the thousand lifetimes we've shared.

Upon the River of Light

Upon the River of Light,
our souls travel as constant
companions in Oneness,
on this magnificent journey
to the Sea of Love,
swept to where all Souls meet.

We have listened to what is Sacred,
staying on the narrow Path of Truth,
as upon the Earth we choose to travel,
barefoot upon God's tender ground.

We listened to the whispers of ancient trees,
the wings of eagles high above the clouds,
the wondrous words of the Four Winds,
the sweet Silence all around us, everywhere.
And seven thousand songs came in answer,
to all the Questions we had Inside.

Walk Slowly

Walk slowly on the wet sand,
keeping your eyes on the horizon,
your heart feeling everything as
pure Light.

Your body, like bare-wire electricity.
Your senses, aware of all life.
Feeling everything, as the first time,
your steps retracing, back to the Divine.

Listen to this humble song and explore,
the underbelly of precious words.
Taste this journey to the fragile truth,
this beating drum of heart,
and the soft skin of my soul.

And, in the silent pause of breaths,
within the deepest part of you,
find the promise, the gateway
we all seek, to the Universal Soul.

When Words Turn to Song

We walk this tiny planet for such a short time.
We reach for ghosts and climb upside down,
most of us bloodied, mixed up and out of rhyme,
till a miracle or sublime circumstance comes around.

Then life, as we have known it, seems to melt away.
Time finally stops us in a perfect forever slow-motion.
Colors never seen, come alive turning night into day.
And if you whisper words of intention to the Universe,
You may discover how God turns words into song.

Without Reservation

I am overcome with emotions
that draw from a wellspring of love.
I am filled with a joy blessed by God,
and I am so euphoric, knowing her Gifts.
Having searched my entire life to find this place,
this home, that tells me this seeking is at end.
My soul imagined this day would come suddenly,
and everything I am, would be enough and all she needed.

And now, as I stand at the threshold of my longing and desire,
like Icarus, I must decide to fly and burn too close to the sun,
for my love has shared her secret openly,
and in this decisive forthcoming of our journey,
her wings are tethered, still bound to another Sun.

And if I jump into the vastness of this promising bliss,
it is without the knowing, that she can and will soar with me.
I must be brave and courageously jump into this star-struck night.
And pray this woman, this goddess and magnificent creation,
will choose to take this leap, and fly,
without reservation into a new life!

Chapter 2
Interiors, Landscapes
and the Sea

A Semi-Strange Valentine Rhyme

Traveling on this bus bound for Bellingham,
now less than a hundred miles away,
I press my face against the cold glass,
and stare out the window's landscape,
flashing by at 70 miles per hour now.

And I am wondering how you are doing,
since I didn't get to spend time comforting you
as we mingled with so many people
most of whom I didn't know, but wanted to.
I wanted to touch others in the greater circle -
all those strangers sweetly touched by *her,* too!

And now images of Tomo and Kathy stare back at me,
my face still pressed against the cold pain,
and the bus rolls on- no real destination in its wheels-
well maybe, the highway seems like its friend.
And I just keep breathing in deeply,
letting in what remains joyful and fresh as possible,
and in the pushed out-breath, release what's lost.

I remember that downtown San Francisco balcony,
on that Saturday, when we shared a smile,
passing glasses of wine to ease the sting.
And I told each of you, 'I love you' one way or another,
hoping that might ease our troubled souls.

And right then, and maybe more now,
I realized how much of you is divine.
Your heart is bigger than the full moon.
Your love for your sisters shone brightly,
as you kept company in the fading sun.
And I watched you. No, in truth, *saw you more clearly,*
and was so grateful that you were in all our lives.

I can feel God touching my hand softly,
as the wheels stop. And, stepping off the bus,
releasing the valve pounding in my head,
and caught off guard, at the end of my journey north,
I listen deeply and watch how souls move about,
in and out, of this crazy world.
The angel you are, should not go unnoticed,
on any day, but certainly not on Valentine's Day!

Alexandria

I watch the desperate sun cross
the vast expanse of desert
sitting in the pockets of pleasure
propped up against the old pharaoh's pyramid.

The dominant greens and browns
blush the horizon of sea
and Alexandria, like an over-ripened fruit
lies before me like a historical landscape
of lovers and orgy and iridescent sea.

In the mirrors and masks there is
the smell of disorder and decay
Gnostic gestures of intrigue
hang like lanterns on hot sticky nights.

Alexandria, dripping in aquarelle sketches
of lovers, incapable clocks of emotions
outdistanced by the churn of time.

And she waits for you, there
at the edge of white sand memories
and phosphorescent seas.

A Room of My Own Making

A room in which several plants
stretch out leaves and flowers
to photosynthetic light,
their roots fastening too tightly to escape.

Tattered books blanket the walls
with unspoken words of pain and sorrow.
Old and timeless paintings hung carelessly,
revealing mysteries to those with translucent eyes.
Mobiles dance in kaleidoscopic waves,
crowded around this room of sentimentality.

Idle paint and brushes meant for inspiring canvas,
patiently wait to capture landscapes of the sea.
One open, but silent window, suddenly offers up a voice,
"I am lost in a distant room of my own making,
amidst paper and pulp words I cannot deliver"

Amsterdam in the Rain

Nighttime jazz playing on an old phonograph, soft and low,
and it's raining in Amsterdam this cool Sunday night.
We toured two museums and St. Nicolas Kirk Church
all in one day, and now damn I just want to chill.

Watching my mind rewind and playback softly
all those marvelous and unique expressions of art,
as the rain comes down like soprano saxophone notes,
bringing a cold and gentle cleansing to this amazing place.

And my better Self starts to rise slowly out of the stories
about heart and soul that's guiding the "groove control buttons"
tapping out a smooth-jazz kind of stick drumming against Night.
I pulled up on the couch, and let all the glorious day refresh itself
while my heart turns West and smiles hello, still missing you.

Early Morning on a Golden Gate Bus

Out the window, to my left,
the powerful sun rose easily,
all in a storm and burst of red.
Out the window to my right,
the moon in its subtlety now,
cloaked in fog and yellow-white,
dances with the sun for a moment,
then undresses effortlessly into the sea.
And it reminds me, in this blissful silence,
how amazing life is, and willingly can be,
as it telegraphs all its wondrous connections,
and brings God, gloriously into and out of me.

At the Riverhouse

The sun always comes to an end too soon in November.
The boardwalk below me runs directly to the water's edge.
The Petaluma River is blue-grey in the shadow light of winter,
and the "Whoville" rooftops are still basking in the fading light.

I stare out the corner window where the river joins the San
Pedro Bay.
And then, my eyes look east toward Mt. Diablo, and the
"one twenty-four".
I remember two years ago, and how my world was always
summer-sky blue,
as I return to the warmth of her *surprise*, and those amazing
green eyes.

While the sun continues to shut down, slow and quietly,
I muse on her splendidness, being present to her delight;
the way she stirred my soul, the softness of her skin,
her passionate kisses, and now, after over forty-five years,
she's brought the fireworks I always knew would come.
And now, I easily recognize I could never again be fully alive,
without the magnificent light and grace of her love.

For Mario Who Made Me See

A fixture in his study.
A watch piece to chain him down.
A mirror is half-reflecting,
half collecting dust.
A stereoscope and postcards,
of the Panama Canal.
Posters of Paris and
matches from all the fine hotels.
A hand-crafted mahogany table,
supporting English breakfast tea cups.
The chessmen are idle, lacking company.
A transfigured chair by the fire.
Sailing to Byzantium upon his knee.
A rug worn thin from pacing,
pale from years of service,
the weave of a miscalculated destiny.
Weather is a mere convention,
collecting round his fragile lips.
A round tear slides down his cheek slowly,
and he waits in silence for tomorrow's pension check.

Getting Past the Rain and Sun

In the silences between the rain and trees,
I drop down the half-finished book and climb
outside my boyish pride, headlong in the wind.

The rain cleanses my soul and hides
the water filling my eyes,
as I sort through lost dreams,
and the stinging vibrations of this curving space.

I remember watching you reading so many books of poetry-
Sexton, Levertov and Plath, and others that touched us both.
You were only twenty-something, strutting in too high a heel.
turning box cars into building as you walked the tracks.

And when another day, the Earth had spun, I found you
back inside our flat, lost again in books and fairytales.
I looked up from my own stories, and there you were,
more radiant than the afternoon sun, flooding all over you.
I knew then, I could never truly get past all the nouns of You.

How do I Bring Back that Boy?

How do I bring back that boy
you used to love so innocently?
Where do I stand, so you see my eyes
are speaking to you with the truest light
that made your heart so easily surrender?
And where is the uncontested freedom
that allowed your soul to soar?

And how does one turn broken promises
or keep doubt and fear from a tender heart?
How can I turn this gray cloud atmosphere
back into sparkling sun of innocent trust?
Perhaps you'll realize slowly over time
there is a safe place in my arms again.
And maybe once more, I'll be your boy?

Jumping into the Past

I jumped into the past,
a prisoner of my own words.
A memory almost faded,
brought back to life in a flash of light
by a child of the Seventies,
who painted magical words.
She touched my soul
in the quiet of another world,
when we were still gentle, soft and still.

How had she sampled the deepest part of me,
with just a casual glance?
How could she still hold this power, finding me again,
like a sailor lost at sea, after all these years?
And why gift me the elixir of this potent blissfulness,
I unknowingly, was starving to taste, just once?

Bringing back a spark to light the fire of spiritual dance,
before the tender ashes of forgetfulness had past.
She returned to me from some distant constellation,
with her soft whispers of love and remembrance,
replenishing the sweet memories of my thirsty tongue.

Sailing to Kauai

The vast white sailcloth was made
from silk of the white buffalo hair.
The wooden hull crafted
from the finest timber of ancient redwood forests.
The timeless navigations
made from intuition and astrological charts,
were painted flawlessly over 46 years ago,
far from the Pacific Coast.

The crew of two, had studied the winds
consistently for as many years.
And, after hauling the small craft
across the great sands of all those years,
they set sail, ceremoniously launching their boat of dreams,
with such joy and abandon of heart
to the distant island of Kauai.

After two long treacherous years of storms and ferocious winds,
the tiny brutally sturdy boat reached shore in 2020.
The two sailors, exhausted and barely able to crawl ashore,
with such beautiful release,
fell into the sands of their lifelong dream.
They wrapped themselves in each other's weary bodies,
knowing their god-inspired journey, was now complete.

Night Swimming Alone

Swimming in his longing,
in this cold azure sea of love,
he knows, "I'm not dreaming, and yet
this lightness of breath
is fueled by the moon on this luminous night."
The constant thrill in each arm stroke
and the pure joy when skin and water collide.

Hours now, no longer feeling hands or feet,
his face is cold, almost frozen in the foam.
But his eyes stay fixated on what's still in reach,
and there in the short distance left,

the answer, that unmistakable delight,
miraculously waiting on the shore.

The Canvas of Delight

A new canvas, white and freshly prepared,
stretched across a wooden frame just right,
is waiting patiently at dawn's early keeping.

Paint brushes and acrylic paints, like soldiers,
stand awaiting the novice, beckoning his strokes.
He closes his eyes and memories flood in delight.
Her eyes sparkle light diamonds in front of him,
but were they brown or blue-green emeralds in flight?

He swims in the fragrance of her melodic voice,
and remembers the soft and tender white skin,
revealed just below a fan-like oriental dress.
He approaches the canvas and wants to run away,
his imagination much more magnificent than his strokes.
But, joy can pass you by, like a breeze or dust so easily,
if you don't show your heart in the great moments of risk,
and brave your love into a world that awaits your paint.

The Mystery of Love

What is this wondrous waterfall
the wild submerging into surrender,
when our souls fall into the waters of love?

And how can one still be so thirsty for another,
when they are already drunk on this divine passion,
having tasted the exquisite pleasures of another's lips?

And what of the heart in these wild storms,
and the whitecaps of relentless waves?
Are we taking turns diving for magical pearls,
in this beneficent ocean of Love?

When I Owned Your Words

When I owned your words,
a new breeze blew through my hair,
my eyes turned a little bluer,
my forehead and temples relaxed
and a smile turned upon my lips.

When I owned your words,
I heard the branches sing,
and saw the nest and sunshine
in the tree.

When I owned your words,
I felt the thrill of recognition,
the blast of fresh air,
the flush of cinnamon and cayenne,
the truth whispering near my ear,
and the sky was full of bright white clouds.

Chapter 3
Nature

The River Story

The colors of day subside around the River,
and I begin to breathe in recognition,
the quiet knowing and stillness of solitude.

Awakening to the transformative consistency of Night,
I recognize this River as an old Friend.
And I bow in a sacred ancient greeting, Namasté.
All the while, my soul is looking to the East,
leaning into the heart of my beautiful beloved friend,
wanting only to bathe in the midnight oil of her Soul!

A Beacon to an Ancient Boat

Every time,
and all at once,
I hear the calling of her voice,
the triumphant water bells,
that rich and brilliant light ashore,
the powerful center of a safe harbor,
a beacon to my ancient boat, damaged by storms,
but courageously afloat. And every time I have
the strength to listen, in tender whispers, riding
the ocean winds, she brings me home time and time again.

A Perfect Pair

These two Redwoods stand tall in magnificence
reaching toward Heaven, their strong wings uplifted
and yet, just as strongly rooted in the rich Mother Earth.

Root and Branch, Sun and Earth,
bound together in friendship and love,
connected to all that nourishes Life.

We too are united by all that creates and endures,
separated only by our last thought, or most recent dream.
Intertwined by love and our exhilaration we touch,
sensing God's creation. Paradise still in the making,
we fulfill that timeless awakening, a Perfect Pair.

A Small and Sturdy Boat

I offer this small and sturdy boat of love
for the storms you face with each passing moon.
It is woven of wood from the great eternal forests,
built, slat by slat, by the mighty hands of ancient gods.
It will not sink, no matter how hard the ferocious winds blow.
It will weather each and every unexpected strike from the
　　darkness.
And always I will be the oarsman, the watchman and rudder.
Each, so you will easily cross the storms in any ocean or sea,
until finally, you reach the white sands of love's endless shore.

Déjà Vu Ascent

And now, we can equally accept
there are no more forgotten trails.
No more rock markers, nor icy steps.
Gone too, the passionate torches from our past.
But the signposts we now continually receive,
surely brighten our soul's journey through the dark.

And in the morning, again, we begin anew
the miracle of this déjà vu ascent,
this climb we solemnly agreed to attempt,
before time began and all souls were one.
I hold out my hand, delighted once again,
asking you to hold on tightly, as we ascend.

The Friendship of Wind and Majestic Oak

From the first time, they smiled,
laughed deep inside their trunks,
they felt each other and realized
the perfect simplicity of branches,
two trees, dancing in joy with the wind.

And somewhere, in between the thought,
and the slow utterance of misplaced words,
they, like the majestic trees, slowly realized
what connection was, deep within their souls,
where the warm breeze tenderly weaved a love-story
throughout the intoxicating seasons come and gone.

Still, as the cold winter winds cut sharply through bark
and skin over the difficult, long-passing years,
as they grew more brittle and their limbs curled,
and gnarled like those two majestic oaks,
they never forgot that deep-rooted passion,
or the promises of love, friendship, trust and hope.
Isn't it wonderful, if only once, to have such a friend?

How Hard, How Cruel

How hard and ever-long
these fall days go on and on,
when all I can do is softly whisper
 the melody of this near-silent song.
How cruel and cold the blue skies feel,
when all I want is to feel her bright sun,
 and taste a love from which I cannot run.

How hard the days go on when I look backwards,
and lost in the tender moment like water and sand,
lingering in the shadows of her Mitchell-like voice.
How unkind the pinks and purples of sunset have become,
no longer finding the joy, once filled by those mesmerizing eyes!

In the Midst of It All

Standing in the midst of Ocean and Wave,
I reach toward Sky in prayer and affirmation,
filling my lungs with the sacred song of belonging.

And feeling so divinely connected,
amidst white caps of awakening,
my heart writes such tender messages within its welling.
My body lifted towards Sun
from what rises within the deep of me,
and my soul cries out joyfully, as I breathe in the Sea and Sky.

The Song of Love

(for little girls of any age)

The seedling broke through the ground
with great effort and immense joy,
and began to sing passionately
in praise of rain clouds and sun,
though never losing the deep bond
with the soil in which it was born.

Was it to become a flowering plant,
or grow into a wild majestic oak?
It didn't really matter; just breaking free,
and breathing in the miraculous air
was so thrilling to the tiny plant,
that it was filled with pure delight.

And on the first day of the seedling's singing,
a young village maiden hiking in the meadow
was enthralled by the beautiful song she heard,
and discovered to her joyous astonishment,
it was the little seedling bringing forth this rhapsody.

And in the short days and long nights that followed,
daily, she would tend to and nurture this tiny plant
with such loving care and tender devotion.
It became the most magnificent rose bush on Earth.
And when the rose bush brought forth its first blossom,
it was the richest in a color of splendid red.
Its fragrance almost magical, and
in a voice, sweet as any angel ever spoke,
the rose bush offered its first flower
to this young maiden in a brilliant song of love.

The Flower that Passes

Love is the flower that passes,
so selflessly, between you and me.
Love is the infinite reception of Light,
that forever brings your fiery lips,
slowly, ever closer to mine.

Water is the Way

Water falls from the Skies,
while the Sun pierces
the billowing white clouds.
And we search for rainbows,
signposts of our magnificent love.

We flow as two intertwined rivers,
to the vast ocean of our dreams.
Sun and Moon to light our path,
and the Grace of God guides the Way.

In the Waters of Life

We can float uncomfortably,
perhaps tread water impatiently,
tiring incessantly in the deep.
And eventually sink in our own bitter despair,
as we grapple with the utter inconvenience of Life.

Or, we can swim magnificently, and triumphantly,
fully engaged in the graceful flow of this life.
When we do, our view moving forward shifts dramatically,
and we are wet with joy, and constantly blessed
with alluring possibilities and beautifully new perceptions.

Chapter 4
Passion

I Can Feel It Still

Oh, what joy, when I touched your skin,
felt my lips press against yours,
pierced your essence with my flesh.
Lying next to you and feeling everything imaginable -
Body, Mind, Heart and Soul, completely fulfilled.
I can feel it still, all over my body again and again.

Thought I had my knowing of Love, before that day,
now I've learned there is a magic beyond this realm.
This ecstasy, this divine thrill,
has brought all my castle walls down.
I am whole, so alive, so mesmerized near you.

And when suddenly separated,
I feel such a need to taste your soul.
Lost without you this night, I drop to my knees,
praying you'll know, all this love that's just for you.

56.3

How can it be that this number drives me so crazy?
How is it that my body is ignited with such desire?
I feel I could leap the distance in a single bound, and
I sense the possibility of your touch so tantalizingly near.
Never has my soul wanted to jump into my car more.
The engine is ready. My tank full of fuel.
Hands grip the wheel; transmission thrown into reverse.
I back to the edge of the driveway,
and stop with devastating remorse and hesitation.

Everything inside pleads me "drive to those promises!"
Imagining all these desires will finally meet their match,
but the realization of this dream too, must once again pass.
And back into the garage the engine quietly shuts down.
Perhaps another night my soul will finally take flight.

A King's Treasure Chest

And you, with those sparkling emerald eyes,
stole me from the dark nights of too many years.
It was you that turned those painful tears
into magnificent pearls and diamonds clear.
And now at last, I've bent mighty Ulysses' bow.
A true King, I can now claim your heart,
and give you all the pleasures you desire,
the full abundance of this treasure chest.

Anticipation, Again at my Door

Today I realized how wide this river courses through me,
and how perfectly divine this magnetic current runs to me.
Tonight, settled in, I wait in stillness and quiet mindfulness,
filled with an unimaginable Love and magnificent Peace,
knowing that soon, my greatest treasure will soon be at my
    door.
Tonight, when the world is soft and the stars cast their
    warm light,
I will deliciously taste the sweet bliss from my lover's kiss,
and, pulling her into the range of this constant longing,
once again, I'm blessed by a feeling of pure exquisiteness.

As the Night Moves

And so, the night moves from early to late,
from easy, to can't wait.
And I wonder how it is with you?

Do you share this same sense that I'm feeling?
Do you catch your breath,
wanting something more to fill your night?

Are you wanting to be alone,
with not a single distraction?
Wanting to have that singular rush
through your skin?
Does your pulse increase, temperature rise?
Is there a sense of urgency imminent in your mind?

Is this solitarily unique, or am I right
in recognizing you are exactly there,
wanting this intimate connection as much as I do?
Are you wishing to be where you've been in your mind,
over and again, a thousand times?
Or, wanting to be against the tropical breeze,
feeling the wet sand and ocean on your feet?

What will it take to bring you to this beach?
What must I do to signal that I am within reach,
waiting just beyond the white sand,
to come forward and take your trembling hands?
Walk the long concourse of waves, and feel that magic
breath given us to live in a birthday kind of day.

Speak soon Goddess, if this night will be filled with your light,
or if I must roam in the dark shadows of this torture
alone again tonight, left only to find you in my dreams.

At the Depth of this Love

I want to saturate myself
in this magic that is you.
To meet you dancing atop
the rolling waves of green & blue seas.
Then, to float together harmoniously,
as our dreams and souls desire emerge.

I want to forever taste, the essence of you,
and know your soul's longitude and every marker.
I want to dive into this divine spray, and
immerse myself in the limitless ocean of this love.
I pray you'll join me in this sublime mystery.
I want to fully experience your breath on mine,
your electric kisses, the thrill of your mystical touch,
as you open fully, to the ecstatic pleasures
of this everlasting divine dance of Embrace.

Beat the Drums Again

Oh, Heart so full of joy and love,
beat the drums again for this goddess,
who so mightily stirs my ecstatic soul.
Reach out with mystical words,
before her eyes turn away.

Let her experience the intensity
of this steadfast and simple offering.
Crack her tender heart wide open,
and set aflame that delicate soul,
as I lavish these spiritual treasures
unto her open arms, with sacred intent.
Praying now, she will take my hand,
and walk harmoniously to the drumming
of my heart's hallowed song.

Brushing Against my Skin

Did you find me, or was it me who found you?
You brushed effortlessly against my skin like a veil,
touching me softly like an angel or ephemeral mist.
Oh, but your eyes were ablaze with such mystical fire,
your body swimming in a sacred dance,
your lips filled with music I had never felt till then.
Your drumbeat began surging in my heart,
the Divine blushed in waves against my soul,
an unspoken knowing, filled me with anticipation-
my soul's long-awaited connection to this desire.

Breathless

This love I'm feeling,
like none I've ever known,
blossoms deep inside
with the joy of understanding.
This love I breathe in
fills me with newness and expansion,
in every single breath and
embraces all fibers of my being.
Her Moon glows under my skin,
and her Sun burns in every cell.
Her eyes so bright, and forever seeking,
shine a light that touches my soul,
as she reveals the core of her being,
and shares a pathway to sacredness.
I can only surrender to all this magnificent light,
knowing this love will forever leave me breathless.

China Musk

I want to touch you anew
bring the distance into sight
and easily float across
the wingspan of your eyes.

I want to smell you – musty eucalyptus,
alkaline droplets, and China musk.
Not, perpetual roses
and honey-coated underarms.
I want to know you
without any extras.
Just you and your nakedness.

Love's Possession

For her own mysterious reasons,
she allowed me to possess her.
To command her with a smile,
and sail my fleet into her seas.

She shook her waist-long hair,
A delightful shimmering corn-silk affair,
from under that tattered straw hat,
and danced under a wild fiery spell.
Giggling all-the-while, never leaving my eyes,
she dropped her dress and fell in submission.

Dancing Dangerously Close to You

We danced dangerously close.
Our eyes wide open to the moment,
our lips pressed softly together, then hard,
clinging to each other in such a tight embrace.

We were moving slowly in small circles.
Our bodies hot as the summer night.
I was impatient and steaming with desire,
in anticipation of what delicious encounters
awaited us after so many unclaimed years,
and too many unkindled fires, now long passed.

You were so vibrant, smiling so fresh and sweet.
I remember gazing into those green and hazel eyes,
instantaneously realizing, you had brought me fully alive.

Fully Alive

Today is another day
to be fully alive,
living in the movements,
brought on by your tide.

You are sunshine and moonbeams,
washing over me in ecstasy.
Your love, a warm summer rain,
attending to the joy in my heart.
Your breath bringing life to my soul.

I feel the flood of your chemistry,
petals covering my body in endless showers,
filling all my senses completely,
with such a kaleidoscope of amazing delight.

Have Mercy on Me

I wasn't searching, not seeking all of this,
when I found myself driving toward your door.
And I couldn't wait to jump into the flames,
or the fiery world of all you held, burst open.
Didn't know the gifts forged from your powers,
when I drank you in so deeply,
Truly I was spinning like a dervish,
and you were the holy water to my soul.

And you, just keep opening and opening,
offering up the tender parts of your aching soul.
Jumping into the deep was oh so easy then.
I just wanted to swim there freely, and then dive
into the deepest part of your magnificent sea,
never guessing how hard you'd crash into me.
And breaking open my ribs, taking all I offered,
my heart gave everything without a word,
never asking God to intercede.
Never asking, "Have Mercy on Me".
Everything I am, is there for you to receive.

Her Misty Rose

Nothing can bend this steel I have forged for you.
Nothing can break the branches or uproot this joy.
I only have to look out my window now, to the East,
and I am flooded with images of us traveling beyond words,
on the threads of golden light to reach each other in mid-
    flight.

And I think of how many times you have touched my soul,
or how you have taken me into weightlessness again and again.
The blissful pleasure as you unfold your essence so easily.
And your willingness to share all of your passionate desires,
the fragrant surrender and magnificent opening
of that glorious flower, the misty rose.
your body bathing me in the brilliant light of your love.

In Her Light

Lost in the feelings she brings while
walking toward me, her small bare feet,
and that pale blue summer dress,
so tightly pressed against her slender body.
Her eyes teasing, like magical kaleidoscopes,
there on the beach, 200 hundred yards from me now,
while twilight gently embraces the tender night.

I want to run fast as a bullet towards my imagination,
and dive, headlong into all the nuances of her inspiration,
while riding that sensuous wave she brings as long as I can.

I love the overwhelming thrill she brings,
like an electric guitar in a South Carolina Night.
Smiling and laughing she musters a "hello" soft and low,
in a voice that melts my body ever so slowly
like the late spring sun feasting on Idaho snow.

I breathe in, hard as I can and catch
that scent of hair in the tepid Northwestern night air.
And I feed on the glow of her shimmering summer skin,
as she "accidently "brushes by me almost giggling in jest.
Laughing in a familiar tone, with that quick subtle wink,
I am consumed in a fiery joy I know she meant for me to taste.
And without the remorse of so many sad lover laments,
she can't do me any harm beyond my own making,
and my heart is broken fully open in one endless song.

She is my Muse

Watching now, the flow of her gait,
and those curves that bring such delight!
Her face and eyes, her lips and mouth,
and her blond hair gently dusting my skin.

In every place I look,
she has lit a spark,
given more than I ever expected.
Fueling my soul-lark with her divine,
releasing this bliss to verse and rhyme.

She brings my voice alive each day,
fueling it with immeasurable desire.
Oh, what work I have ahead of me now,
to bring forth from deep within,
this lust for expression in my soul.
She *is* my muse and magical flute.

Lost in the Aftermath
of Unparalleled Love

Understanding tender words spoken,
and the acceptance of their utterance,
is so different than the sacred swimming
in the heart's sea of a once-in-a-lifetime love.

Listening to that crackling voice,
and tormented emotions of love,
her tears filling the expansive skies
in unimaginable ways,
is so different than how I see her,
and know this journey of "Us".
Dancing with her left me
with an unshakeable truth and realization.

Looking into those emerald eyes took me
to the place I called the center of joy.
And in that instant, it was so easily clear,
her intention for pure and simple connection.
I knew then, I'd rather travel this path alone
than lose even a day of her tender affection.

Tasting Another Light-Filled Night

She stood there waiting for night,
here in the warm diminishing light.
Along a long gentle white sand beach,
covered majestically in the silent mist,
she was glowing in the soft light.

There in the faint light of a quarter moon,
and a soft and calming ocean breeze,
I saw her for the first time.
Catching me in the net of her hazel-green eyes,
she pressed her soft skin erotically against mine.
She spoke effortlessly, through unspoken words.
And in the mysterious circle of her exquisite light,
I embraced the divine tasting of an unexpected delight.

The Fencer

Don't measure my lover in cold darkness,
against ancient beauties in statuesque marble.
She moves perfectly alive, gliding over stone,
a goddess yes, but not frozen in still-life.

In all ways, she is fluid and soft as water,
as she responds perfectly, in swift radiance,
or syncopated overtures, slow dancing smiles,
that distinctive stance of a calculated pose.

Moving always in sweet surprises of pure delight,
a fencer, her rapier swiftly pierces my open heart.
She leaves me mesmerized and blissfully stoned,
when her advancing motions enter my smallest thought.

The Web of Bliss

Tonight, I am surrendered,
nestled against the soft night.
Held tight in her self-spun web.
Safe in the clutch of sweet tenderness.

No longer seeking nor questioning,
without fear pounding in my chest.
The longing at last subsided,
I am now fully captured,
forever caught in her web of bliss.

Thriving in Her Light

My love thrives in her light.
My body flinches and stirs,
at the sound of her voice.
My joy increases with every sighting.
My heart beats out of rhythm,
waiting hours for that crazy thrill,
a few minutes spent with her funny laugh.

Every time I see her tap on WhatsApp,
I feel an excitement that electrifies.
With just the thought or promise of a kiss,
my soul flies and I'm dizzy, out of breath.
I can almost taste what I cannot manifest.
And when, at last, she arrives at the park,
Nothing could bring me greater joy,
than the sparkle in her emerald eyes.

Watching from a Bluff

I want to touch you like the wind,
in the short distances between us.
Float across the wingspan of your eyes,
then sink into a dimple brand new.
How I'd love to gently pull myself up,
by the curls hanging round that slender neck.
I want to smell you when your undone and wet.

I want to know you undressed, without embellishments
or misleading blemishes of what was lost.
I love the imperfections of your approaching nakedness.
I like your unprotected-ness,
and the fabulous canopy of flowers
that flourish when you walk into any room.
I want to be contained, wrapped inside,
those energetic smiles and sweet lips.

I feel the flurries of your fiery eyes,
dismissing my hesitation with each glance,
overwhelmed in anticipation, this piercing of heart,
and trusting you in ways only my soul,
lost in this moment, can truly comprehend.

When Words Scream Across the Page

Thanks for the inspiration of pen attacking page,
with veracity, determination and such velocity.
Imagine having this feeling of freedom,
of absolute joy!
Simply in this moment,
your eyes, your smile and your hair,
bring me to this foundational place,
this glimpse into the outer edge of eternity.

My left-hand shakes with relentless pleasure,
and I am not willing to stop its flow.
Words spring onto the page at an alarming rate,
as if there is only this moment in time.
What more can life offer than this
exhilaration in this fantastic space?

The glow and fragrance lingers in thought,
never to be matched in words by my pen.
Heat, vibration and ecstasy, matching the fire,
that passion of being holds me,
locked in love.

Words run across the page,
like contrails writing across the twilight sky.
Night stars and a brilliant moon,
leave me so caught up in this place.
I might never leave, never cease to be,
never feel anything more perfect in my heart.

Your Love

Your love pours into me now,
as magnificent fluid Light.
Your green emerald eyes meet mine,
and sparkle with pure magical delight.
You fill my heart and soul so deeply,
with an unimaginable taste of bliss.
You awaken a hunger so vibrant and rare,
as I breathe in all textures and hues,
immersed in the ocean of colors of you.

Wicked, Unwanted Spell

The light has faded many hours now.
Darkness surrounds me like an unwanted blanket,
on yet another hot and endless summer night.
And I am bare. My soul naked and torched.

I search for a pill or some bud to calm the banging sounds,
to find my balance, seeking to resolve this dull aching pain,
and these terrible under-the-skin longings.
They seem the same, so late at night.
And I want her lips, her touch, her curves all over my skin.

How did I get this way, so imprisoned in this spell so quick?
What magic potion? What incantation or charm was invoked?
My body is on fire and my skin feels electrified.
And I have nowhere to take shelter,
no cave in which I might hide.
But, this wild man inside,
has nothing but desire, and will not shrink.

Dreaming of Her Again

For days now, I've been dreaming of her,
filled with a sense of bewilderment and awe,
lost in the tangle of her long sweet golden hair.
Scented with a thousand wishes, her body speaks
in a sign language, quite familiar to my speechless soul.

Joyously, that fragrance floats constantly in my mind,
feeding my heart and speaking to my waiting quill.
Like an ancient metaphor left entombed in the Sacred Inner
    World,
she comes calling to all my fiery senses every sleepless night.
Ten thousand dreams floating on iridescent "gossamer wings",
I lay down all hesitation, opening my arms in exquisite
    anticipation.

I love Your Splendidness

I love you in silk and soft velvet,
but even more, in nothing but skin.
I love your gorgeous long flowing hair,
especially when its curly and just a tad wet.
I love your amazing green and hazel eyes,
and how they reveal the Universe when I gaze inside.
I love the way you taste and your sweet mesmerizing smell.
I love saying your name over and over to my soul's delight.
I love the thrill of your naked body's response to sensuous touch.
I love catching you when you're off-balance, about to fall,
and soothing your tears, when the pain of life makes us small.
I love knowing you are my muse, confidant, soul mate and
best friend.

I love that you have given me your heart and let me in so deep,
and

I love the uniqueness of your Light, your Love and splendid
Soul!

My Summer Dream

Now that I have found you in my dreams,
you will be the breath in this poem.
You, with that curly hair you swear is wavy,
and those eyes that are so very deep,
I call postcard ocean blue.
I see you with that quick smile,
 and know the essential motion of your soul.

I am reminded of the this and that of you,
the insignificant gestures you toss about,
the flip flop glide of your shoes,
the way you brush your hair from your face,
the way the ocean touches your soul so sweet,
and how you give yourself to a sunset,
each time it seems brand new!

I like the sense of your being so light,
and the way you taste the world.
I like the precision of your shoeless steps,
your long body coming down the tight hall,
especially when you're naked or barely dressed.

And when you're under a waterfall in the afternoon sunshine,
I want to touch you like I was water and sun,
move across you like a San Francisco Fog.
I want to float like ice, past your wanting eyes,
just before slipping into the dimples of your thighs.
I want to find my body constantly encountering your nights,
to rhyme with those erect nipples,
and fall speechless into that soft body noun.

How much better I feel, and it truly is,
when I'm over your body and soft smooth skin,
lost in the arch of your long slender back.
But I'm lost in the night, twisting and turning over phantoms,
arms encircling shadows of historic dreams.
My body and mind are lost in you – leaf and tree,
and you are my summer dream.

Can I Begin to Make You See?

Can I begin to bring all *this,* to you again,
to reach the depth of my soul once more,
and give you every fiber of me, unconditionally?
Can I make you see how ferocious this river of desire,
has brought about this flood of absolute surrender,
and given form to the magnificent bliss you've brought me?

Saturday Morning South City

Waking up next to your green eyes,
I want these feeling to last lifetime.
And, next to your warm exquisite lines,
I know nothing could ever satisfy more.

Waking up next to your morning smiles,
multi-colored sunsets fill my skies.
Am I still dreaming, swimming and frolicking,
like a dolphin in last night's ecstasy?

I feel my steel pulse rise and surge once again.
Feel the passion, of your Lion King's knocking
at the sacred entry of your temple's doors.
I offer you all these affections.
Beyond still awaits the mysteries of my soul.

Acknowledgments

Thanks so much to all of you who have helped shape this little book of poetry.

Thanasis Maskaleris and Nanos Valaoritis, my amazing college professors, who taught me so much about living out loud. Margot Meyer, who taught me about higher love. Elaine Pettinella. who encouraged my writing through her love and gentle ways. Mark Nepo, who inspires me every day in so many ways. The Evolving Man Men's Community, who held me accountable for much of the final steps of this journey to publishing. Robbi Dunham, who taught me compassion and unconditional love. Robert Girard, who taught me words like obstreperous and recalcitrant. Geoff Laughton, whose friendship and wisdom have kept me afloat so many times. My dad, Joey Francis, who taught me how to be a gentle man. My son Ian, who has the magical gift of laughter, and who's passion for music matches my own. Katharina Gerlach, without whose help, this project of love would still be collecting dust.

All of the muses of my life, that dwell both in nature and the flesh. And to you OCG, whose light and beauty remain unmatched.